VANGUARD SERIES

EDITOR: MARTIN WINDROW

Fallschirmpanzerdivision
'HERMANN GÖRING'

Text by BRUCE QUARRIE

Colour plates by JEFFREY BURN

squadron/signal publications

Published in 1978 by
Osprey Publishing Ltd
Member company of the George Philip Group
12–14 Long Acre, London WC2E 9LP
© Copyright 1978 Osprey Publishing Ltd

First published in the USA in 1978 by
Squadron/Signal Publications, Inc.,
3461 East Ten Mile Road,
Warren, Michigan 48091.

ISBN 0 85045 124 8

Filmset by BAS Printers Limited,
Over Wallop, Hampshire
Printed in Hong Kong

Anyone researching the 'Hermann Göring' Division
must acknowledge, as does the author, a major debt to
Roger James Bender and George A. Petersen, authors
of *Hermann Göring—from Regiment to Fallschirmpanzerkorps*
(R. James Bender Publishing, 1975). Other invaluable
sources consulted during the preparation of this book
include, among others, *Fallschirmjäger* by R. Böhmler
and W. Haupt (Verlag Hans-Henning Podzun, 1971)
and W. G. F. Jackson's *The Battle for Italy* (Batsford,
1967). The author is further indebted to Werner
Haupt for his help and encouragement at the
Bundesarchiv, Koblenz—the source of all photographs
used in the book; to David List for copies of 13
(British) Corps intelligence reports from the Public
Records Office; and to his wife Linda, for taking a
holiday at the right time so that he could finish writing
the manuscript!

This book is dedicated to Martin, who learned that
parachute jumping is not as easy as it looks . . .

Men of the Wach-Kompanie parade with the standard presented to the unit in September 1933. This has a grass-green ground and scroll; white swastika, 'grenades', wreath and central disc; black eagle, brown arrows; gilt beak, talons, swordhilt and arrowheads. The photograph was taken at Göring's famous residence, Karinhall. (Bundesarchiv 638/4287/19)

Origins and Early History

Hermann Göring, Hitler's corpulent and sycophantic Minister of the Interior and later Reichsmarschall of the Luftwaffe, was one of those men who simply had to have a finger in every pie. The result was his creation of a Luftwaffe field unit with its own recruiting standards, training and uniform, independent of either the Army or the SS, and under Göring's personal overall command. The division had an unhappy history initially: of their fighting record in Russia in 1941, von Mellenthin* says that they were 'a creation which had no sound military foundation—the rank and file paid with their lives for this absurdity'. This judgement is, perhaps, over-harsh, as we shall see; but certainly in its early campaigns the unit suffered from inadequate tactical leadership through being officered mainly by Luftwaffe personnel with no real grasp of ground warfare. Only after it was virtually wiped out in Tunisia in 1943 did it receive experienced leadership in the form of officers transferred from the Army. But from that date a remarkable transformation took place, and within a year it had grown to the strength and status of a fully fledged Panzer division which gave the Allies serious problems in Italy and stubbornly resisted the Russians in the closing stages of the war. Thus, although it took only a minor part in the glamorous blitzkrieg campaigns of the early war years, and was engaged predominantly in heavy defensive fighting for the remainder of the period, the 'General Göring' Regiment and its successors—

'Hermann Göring' Brigade, Division, Panzerdivision, Fallschirmpanzerdivision and finally Fallschirmpanzerkorps—fulfilled the tasks allotted to it with courage and élan, and well merits special consideration in any study of the fighting troops of the Third Reich.

* * *

Göring, who had been appointed Prussian Minister of the Interior on Hitler's accession to power at the beginning of 1933, immediately set about forming an élite police unit whose principal task was to seek out and exterminate Communist 'enemies of the State'. Known initially as Polizeiabteilung zbV 'Wecke' (after its first commander, Major Wecke, who was executed in Prague in 1947), the 414-man strong unit came into being on 25 February 1933 and thus antedates its comparable élite units in the SS and Army, the 'Leibstandarte Adolf Hitler' and 'Grossdeutschland', which were formed in the autumn of 1933 and 1934 respectively. The Abteilung rapidly established a reputation for brutal efficiency in its raids on workers' quarters in Berlin, with dozens of arrests to its name. In July of the same year the Abteilung was retitled Landespolizeigruppe 'Wecke' zbV and in September was presented with a special standard by Göring who, with his eyes on the future, stated his intention to transform the Prussian police force into a 'sharp-edged weapon' which he would be able to deliver to the Führer 'when the day comes for us to fight our external enemies'.

Panzer Battles (University of Oklahoma Press, 1956).

3

In December 1933 the unit was again re-christened, this time as Landespolizeigruppe 'General Göring', with Oberstleutnant Friedrich Jakoby taking command in June 1934. When general conscription was introduced in Germany in March 1935, the unit was given the more martial title Regiment 'General Göring' and, from 1 October of the same year, it was incorporated into the Luftwaffe. At this time the regiment comprised two Jäger battalions plus a motorcycle and a pioneer company, and shortly thereafter it also acquired two guard of honour (Wach) companies and a light flak Abteilung (= battery; 'Abteilung' is a rather vague German military term which can mean 'battery', 'battalion', 'department' or simply 'unit').

Göring was interested in the possibilities of parachute units and, in January 1936, the 1st Jäger Battalion, under the command of Major Bruno Bräuer (who won the Knight's Cross in Holland in 1940 and was subsequently executed after the war, in Greece), together with the regimental pioneer company, was sent to the Döberitz training area to begin parachute training. The remainder of the regiment was sent to the Altengrabow training area for more general military instruction. In August of the same year Oberstleutnant Jakoby handed over command to Major Walter Axthelm, who later rose to the rank of General, became the commander of the I Flakkorps and won the Knight's Cross in Russia.

In many fields, German military thinkers were not always the first to realize the possibilities of a weapon, but were often the first to recognize and exploit its true practical potential in battle. The Soviet army had been experimenting with parachute forces since 1928, and revealed their techniques to the world in 1936 at a demonstration involving a thousand parachutists. Göring had been aware of these experiments for some time, and the Army was also interested. The result was an

Part of the motorcycle company on manoeuvres; the longship device can be seen on the door of the SdKfz 16 medium radio car in the foreground. (Bundesarchiv 639/4293/32)

amalgamation, with the four companies of the former 1st Jäger Battalion, Regiment 'General Göring', forming the training cadre of the 1st Fallschirm-Infanterie-Bataillon, under command of Major Richard Heidrich—who made his first jump at the age of 41. The Army had organized its first Fallschirm company in the autumn of 1936 and both units took part in the large-scale manoeuvres at Mecklenburg in 1937, which greatly impressed Hitler. However, the men of the 'General Göring' Regiment were not directly involved. The four Jäger companies and the pioneer company were divorced from their parent units in March 1938 and, with additional Army companies, were reformed as the 1st Fallschirmjäger Regiment under Generalmajor Kurt Student in July. This left the 'General Göring' Regiment as a simple flak (anti-aircraft) unit for the time being, with one heavy and two light flak Abteilungen, a reinforced searchlight (Scheinwerfer) Abteilung, guard and training battalions, and an armoured train (Eisenbahn-Flak-Batterie) under command. In addition there was also a detached light flak unit appointed to provide AA defence for Hitler's headquarters, and a personal bodyguard for Göring himself.

Entry requirements for the 'General Göring' Regiment were highly selective. Recruits had to be a minimum of 1.68 metres tall and between the ages of eighteen and twenty-five; moreover, they had to be German citizens of 'Aryan' ancestry, unmarried, with a clean record, no criminal convictions and good physique. They also had to swear that they would 'always and openly' support the Nazi regime. Enlistment was for a period of twelve years. Enlistment in this élite formation had its advantages, not least of which were the superb barracks at Berlin-Reinickendorf. These had been built under Göring's personal supervision—he was a sybarite to the last!—and included every possible comfort and convenience.

In 1938 the regiment was among those selected to take part in the occupation of Austria, the Sudetenland and Czechoslovakia, but only the 1st (Light) Flak Battery participated in the Polish campaign of September 1939; the remainder of the regiment stayed behind to provide anti-aircraft defence for Berlin and a guard for Göring's headquarters. However, in the spring of 1940 a

Wheel change for one of the 'HG' Regiment's BMW motorcycle combinations. Markings to note are the Luftwaffe numberplate 'WL-379405'; the white unit insignia with a yellow 'hand' indicating by its position on the disc that the vehicle belongs to the 11th Company; and the white longship motif, complete with the legend 'NORGE' on the sail, which identifies a unit which took part in the Norwegian campaign of 1940. (Bundesarchiv 639/4267/14)

special battlegroup comprising one of the guard companies, a 20mm flak battery and a newly created motorcycle (Kradschützen) company, under the command of Major Waldemar Kluge, took part in the Norwegian campaign. Subsequently these units adopted an unofficial Viking ship device which was painted on the sides of their vehicles (see accompanying photo).

Meanwhile the 1st (Heavy) Flak Abteilung, the 4th (Light) and the searchlight Abteilungen had been secretly transferred to the Western Front in October 1939 and, in May 1940, operating under the cover designations of Flak Regiments Nrs 101 and 103, they took part in the invasion of France with Kleist's and Guderian's Panzergruppen. Crossing the River Maas and the Albert Canal, they fought in the Dyle Line breakthrough and participated in the occupation of Brussels. It was during this campaign that the German 8.8cm anti-aircraft gun proved itself in the anti-tank role, the 1st (Heavy) Flak Abteilung of the 'Hermann Göring' Regiment particularly distinguishing itself in the major battle against French tanks in the Mormal Forest.

Following the French campaign the regiment was assigned to static anti-aircraft duties, first on the Channel coast, then in Paris, and finally in Berlin. In early 1941 it was transferred to Rumania to provide defence against Allied bombing raids on the vital Ploesti oilfields. Shortly afterwards it was again transferred, this time to the Eastern Front, and took part in Operation *Barbarossa*—the invasion of Russia. Despite von Mellenthin's comments noted earlier, it fought well in the anti-tank role during the battle of Radziechov and the later encirclements around Kiev and Bryansk. By October 1941 the regiment's records listed no fewer than 324 tanks destroyed and 161 aircraft shot down. Oberst Paul Conrath, who had taken command of the regiment on 1 June 1940, and three other 'Hermann Göring' Regiment officers wore the Knight's Cross by this time—a significant achievement. However, up to this point they had been fighting principally against confused and demoralized opposition, and the real test of their abilities was still to come.

At the end of 1941 the bulk of the regiment returned to Germany for a rest and refit, and in March 1942 Göring ordered its expansion to the size of a brigade. The organization of the 'Hermann Göring' Brigade, as it was re-christened, was as follows: Schützen (Rifle) Regiment 'HG', commanded by Oberst Heyemeier; Flak Regiment 'HG', commanded by Oberstleutnant Hullmann; the special staff elements in Berlin; and a training battalion in Utrecht. The rifle regiment was divided into three battalions, the first of four companies; the second of four companies plus an artillery company; and the third of motorcycle, pioneer, anti-tank and tank companies, plus a workshop section. The flak regiment comprised three battalions numbered 1, 2, and 4 (the third battalion was formed later). The first battalion contained three heavy and three light batteries; the second three heavy, two light and a howitzer battery; and the fourth, stationed in Berlin, three batteries of unknown calibre. In addition, the three companies of the guard battalion were stationed in Berlin. The training battalion in Utrecht comprised a staff company, two rifle companies, a heavy (probably 15cm) infantry gun company, motorized and motorcycle companies, light, heavy and howitzer batteries. German heavy flak batteries normally fielded four 8.8cm guns apiece, light batteries twelve 20mm or nine 3.7cm weapons.

Göring was not satisfied with elevating 'his' regiment to brigade status, however, and barely had it been formed when, without benefit of proper joint training, it was further raised to the size of a division. The accompanying diagram shows the basic divisional organization. In order to increase the brigade to this establishment, 5,000 Luftwaffe volunteers were drafted into its ranks. The Jäger Regiment was formed from the 1st Battalion of Fallschirmjäger Regiment Nr 5 plus the 2nd and 3rd Battalions of Sturm-Regiment 'Koch', all of which had fought in Crete and had subsequently suffered heavy casualties in Russia. These were therefore experienced and battle-hardened troops. The 1st Grenadier Regiment was formed from the 1st and 2nd Battalions of the original Schützen Regiment, with an additional battalion which became Nr 1. The artillery regiment was formed from a third flak battalion, originally designated to form part of Flak-Regiment 'HG'. The other units were formed from reinforced elements of the original brigade. In addition, the guard battalion was strengthened to the size of a regiment, later to be renamed the Führer Begleit Regiment, and the training battalion to the status of a full replacement and training regiment (still based in Utrecht). The

Peaceful duty for one of the division's radio sections in Italy, 1943. They wear Waffen-SS pattern camouflage smocks and helmet covers, but the 'HG' Division's white collar patches can just be seen. (Bundesarchiv 639/4260/30A)

'Hermann Göring' Division 1942–1943

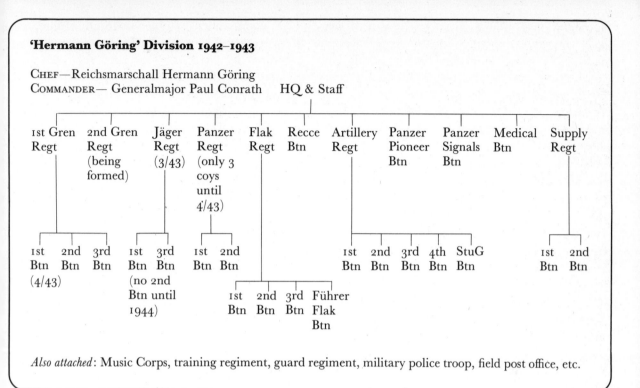

CHEF—Reichsmarschall Hermann Göring
COMMANDER— Generalmajor Paul Conrath   HQ & Staff

- 1st Gren Regt
  - 1st Btn (4/43)
  - 2nd Btn
  - 3rd Btn
- 2nd Gren Regt (being formed)
- Jäger Regt (3/43)
  - 1st Btn
  - 3rd Btn (no 2nd Btn until 1944)
- Panzer Regt (only 3 coys until 4/43)
  - 1st Btn
  - 2nd Btn
- Flak Regt
  - 1st Btn
  - 2nd Btn
  - 3rd Btn
  - Führer Flak Btn
- Recce Btn
- Artillery Regt
  - 1st Btn
  - 2nd Btn
  - 3rd Btn
  - 4th Btn
  - StuG Btn
- Panzer Pioneer Btn
- Panzer Signals Btn
- Medical Btn
- Supply Regt
  - 1st Btn
  - 2nd Btn

Also attached: Music Corps, training regiment, guard regiment, military police troop, field post office, etc.

main body of the new division formed up in Brittany, but in November 1942 the first elements—the seasoned paratroops—were shipped to Tunisia to assist the Afrika Korps, and in December the Flak Regiment and 1st Grenadier Regiment were sent to Italy.

The basic organization within the division was standardized along exactly the same lines as a regular Army Panzer division. The two battalions in the Panzer regiment were each to comprise HQ, two light and one heavy companies, plus workshop and signal sections, etc. The light companies were of three platoons, each of five PzKpfw IIIs plus a further seven tanks in each company HQ; the heavy companies were of only two platoons, each of four PzKpfws IVs plus seven tanks in the company HQ. Each company also included a workshop section for running repairs in the field. The battalion HQ company contained seven tanks plus workshop and signal sections, motorcycle, engineer and anti-aircraft platoons. Naturally, the day to day status within this framework varied considerably according to circumstances and can only be taken as a guide.

As the war continued and new tank designs entered service, the PzKpfw III was largely replaced by various up-gunned and up-armoured versions of the PzKpfw IV in the 'light' companies, while the PzKpfw IV was itself replaced by PzKpfw V Panthers in the 'heavy'. The PzKpfw VI Tiger I and Tiger II were principally issued to the independent Panzer companies and battalions to provide a flexible armoured spearhead, although élite divisions such as the various SS formations, Panzer-Grenadier Division 'Grossdeutschland' and the 'Hermann Göring' Division also received a quota of Tiger Is.

Infantry organization was also standardized, and applied to German airborne units and the 'Hermann Göring' Division as well as to regular Army formations. The smallest tactical unit was the section, comprising an NCO and nine men. Three sections constituted a platoon, and there were four rifle platoons to a company. Each section contained one MG34 or, later, MG42 machine gun. In addition to the rifle sections, each company also contained an anti-tank and a mortar section, each equipped with three guns/mortars. Three such companies made up a battalion with, in addition, a machine gun company and a signal section. Regiments were of three battalions plus an infantry gun company, an anti-tank company, and en-

A group of officers from the Panzer Regiment 'HG', probably in Sicily or Italy, 1943. None wear the white collar patches officially authorized in January 1943. Note the dashing combination of uniforms worn by the officers at left and right—black Panzer jackets worn with the cap, breeches and topboots of the Luftwaffe service dress. The Leutnant at left wears the old-pattern 'General Göring' cuff-title. (Bundesarchiv 639/4274/9)

gineer, signal and reconnaissance platoons. This remarkably well-balanced organization was extremely well equipped with heavy weapons and a high proportion of automatic and semi-automatic small-arms, making it a formidable fighting formation. As the war progressed an increasing proportion of the battalions were motorized, adding greatly to their tactical competence. Initially, however, in the 'Hermann Göring' Division, only the 2nd and 3rd Grenadier Battalions of the 1st Regiment were fully motorized.

Flak regiments were usually of three battalions, as in the 'Hermann Göring' Division. Each battalion comprised twelve 8.8cm and six 20mm guns in three heavy batteries, and a further twenty-four 20mm guns in two light batteries. Eight

60cm searchlights were attached to the light batteries in two units of four. Originally all guns were towed behind trucks or half-tracks, but as the war progressed increasing numbers of the lighter weapons were mounted directly on armoured or unarmoured half-track bodies, and even tank chassis. A Krupp-planned self-propelled armoured 8.8cm flak gun arrived too late to enter service, although the '88' was, of course, mounted in a variety of tanks and self-propelled guns as a tank destroyer.

German artillery regiments were usually four battalions strong in infantry divisions and three battalions strong in Panzer divisions, so the 'Hermann Göring' Division's five-battalion establishment was somewhat extreme. Each battalion comprised three batteries, each of two platoons with two guns and a machine gun per platoon. Two of the batteries were equipped with medium 10.5cm guns, the third with 15cm or, sometimes, 17cm weapons. Once again, as the war progressed, an increasing proportion of these were mounted on self-propelled chassis for greater mobility and speed of action. In addition, the artillery regiments of Panzer divisions also included, as here, an assault gun battalion. These were organized in the same way as the towed artillery battalions, in three batteries, but with three instead of two platoons, each of two guns per battery. The total number of assault guns—predominantly StuG IIIs—in the battalion at full establishment was thus eighteen.

The reconnaissance battalion was seven companies strong, and included an HQ company with armoured cars, two armoured car companies, a motorcycle company, a light car company (Kubelwagens, etc.), and anti-tank, artillery and anti-aircraft companies. The Panzer Pioneer Battalion comprised four companies, one of which was a bridging unit. The Signals Battalion had a radio and a telephone company, and the Medical Battalion was three companies strong.

Tunisia

Not all of these units were sent to Tunisia, however. Except where noted, the bulk of the division had been assembled by October 1942, at which time an experienced Army colonel, Oberst Wilhelm Schmalz, was appointed as an instructor for the raw Luftwaffe recruits. Schmalz was to play an important part in turning the untried human material of the division into an effective fighting force, and was later to take over command from Conrath. Those units which did take part in the Tunisian campaign were formed into a battlegroup under command of Oberst Josef Schmid (who was promoted Generalmajor in March 1943 and awarded the Knight's Cross in June of the same year for his unit's valiant efforts in North Africa). The battlegroup's organization was extremely flexible, and units from other divisions were taken under command, but it ultimately included the 1st and 3rd Battalions of the 1st Grenadier Regiment, under Oberst Ewerth; the 1st and 3rd Battalions of the Jäger Regiment (formed from Fallschirmjäger Regiment Nr 5) under Oberst Koch; the 1st and 2nd Battalions of the Flak Regiment, under Oberstleutnant Hullmann; the 1st Battalion of the Panzer Regiment, under Oberstleutnant Straub; four companies, including one armoured car

company, from the recce battalion; and the signals and medical battalions. Before the division's arrival in Tunisia, the two Fallschirmjäger battalions had been attached to the 10th Panzer Division, along with 'Afrika' Battalion 24, 'Tunisian' Battalion 5, the 14th Company from Panzer-Grenadier Regiment 104 and the 9th Company from Panzer-Grenadier Regiment 69. By mid-March 1943 all these additional units had been taken under command by the 'Hermann Göring' division. A steady trickle of additional units were sent out to reinforce the division almost as quickly as they could be formed, including three more companies for the 1st Grenadier Regiment, the first three companies of the 2nd Grenadier Regiment 'HG' and part of the Panzer Pioneer Battalion. Total strength of the division is thus almost impossible to ascertain accurately, and has been estimated at between seven and eleven thousand men, most of whom were shortly to be marched into captivity.

On 23 October 1942 Montgomery had unleashed his 8th Army's massive assault on the Afrika Korps positions at El Alamein, had broken through, and had thrown the enemy into a headlong —but disciplined—retreat. On 8 November strong American, British and Free French forces landed on the Moroccan coast and headed eastwards towards Tunisia, presenting a deadly threat to the rear of the German and Italian units still fighting in Libya. A company of Fallschirmjäger Regiment 5 was the first ground unit to be flown into Tunis on 11 November, followed by the rest of the regiment's

The white collar patch of the division is clearly seen in this study of an 'HG' sentry—place and date unknown. The pennant, in black and white, denotes a regimental headquarters. (Bundesarchiv 639/4275/16)

two battalions. This swift German reaction was to deny the Allies the prompt victory they had anticipated. The paratroops first encountered Allied patrols on 16 November, and the ferocity of their defence, combined with heavy rain, slowed the Allied advance and finally checked it at Medjez el Bab, some thirty miles south-west of the city of Tunis. South of these positions, Rommel was blocking Montgomery's advance in the well-defended Mareth Line. December and January passed in stalemate, but Rommel then found his lines of communications with von Arnim's 5th Army threatened by two American divisions in the Sbeitla-Gabes area. Leaving part of his forces to hold the Mareth Line, he detached strong armoured units northwards and fell on the 'green' American troops at Kasserine Pass (14–20 February), breaking them and pushing on towards Thala and Tebessa. But Rommel's luck was running out and, when he attempted a similar attack on the 8th Army at Medenine on 6 March, his forces were rudely repulsed. Montgomery outflanked the Mareth positions at the end of

20mm flak cannon being manhandled into position by 'HG' personnel; Italy, 1943. The SS-pattern camouflage clothing is clearly seen. (Bundesarchiv 639/4277/14)

March and a few days later Rommel was ordered home to Germany, leaving command of his unfortunate troops to the Italian General Messe.

In the north, von Arnim's troops, including the 'HG' units of Kampfgruppe 'Schmid', had been holding on valiantly against heavy odds, but the Allied 1st Army finally succeeded in breaking their defences at Longstop Hill at the end of April and the Axis forces in Tunisia were forced back into a defensive perimeter around Tunis itself. The final assault opened on 6 May with a heavy bombing raid followed by a thousand-gun barrage, and by the following night, despite bitter fighting, the Allies had captured Tunis. General von Arnim withdrew his battered troops into the Cap Bon peninsula, a very strong natural defensive position guarded by a double 'wall' of hills with only two 'gates'—at Hamman Lif and Hammamet. But they were not granted time to get established. General Alexander rolled up the foremost defence line in an unprecedented night attack by 6th Armoured Division on 8/9 May, the German command structure broke down, and it became every man for himself. On 12 May the Axis forces in North Africa laid down their arms, including the bulk of the fledgling 'Hermann Göring' Division. Only a few

officers and especially valuable personnel had been evacuated before the final collapse; Schmid himself flew out on 9 May.

8.8cm gun and crew of the 2nd Battery of a flak battalion (red 'hand' on white disc) near Salerno, 1943. A letter 'N' is just visible beneath the insignia in the original, but is unexplained. (Bundesarchiv 639/4282/18)

Sicily

This disaster was far from the end for the 'Hermann Göring' Division. The flak units in Italy and France, the training regiment in Utrecht, and other odd units still existed in more than name, and these formed the core of the 'second' division. Göring ordered an immediate acceleration of the recruitment and training programme and, during summer 1943, units began assembling from all corners of the Third Reich at training grounds in Germany and Holland. By July the bulk of the new division was installed on the island of Sicily as a 'stop-gap' measure against the anticipated Allied invasion. The two grenadier regiments had been re-formed; the Panzer regiment was reorganized and re-equipped in two tank and one assault gun battalions, the flak regiment in two battalions (later three), the artillery regiment in four (later five) battalions,

and other arms of service were brought back to strength. The Führer Flak Abteilung remained on duty at Hitler's East Prussian headquarters, the guard battalion and music corps at Berlin/Reinickendorf, and the training regiment at two stations—Utrecht, as before and Velten near Berlin.

Sicily at this time was dominated by three vital Axis airfield concentrations: that around Castelvetrano in the west; that stretching from Ponte Olivio to Comiso in the south; and that centred around Gerbini just south of Mount Etna. There were also three stretches of coastline where amphibious landings were considered a possibility, each containing ports which would be necessary for the success of an Allied invasion, and each closely related to the airfield complexes: Palermo in the north, Gela in the south and Catania in the east. The new 'Hermann Göring' Division was assigned to the defence of the Gela sector and the Ponte

Oberstleutnant Julius Schlegel (right) and Dom Gregorio Diamare watch the final loading of the crated Cassino treasure at the monastery. Schlegel wears regulation tropical service dress. (Bundesarchiv 729/5/25)

Division and the German 15th Panzer-Grenadier Division, to counter-attack the Gela landings in strength. Conrath advanced confidently and, despite repeated Allied aerial attacks, was positioned to attack by 2pm on the 11th. However, the bravery of his troops was no defence against the massed fire of British and American warships anchored just off the beaches. This bombardment, combined with intense and stubborn fire from the US 1st Armored Division, so thinned his ranks that he was forced to withdraw leaving a third of his tanks and self-propelled guns burning wrecks behind him (including fourteen Tiger Is belonging to the 2nd Company, Tiger Battalion 504, which had been assigned to his command). Nevertheless, the battle had been very close—at one point Conrath had even radioed a jubilant message to the effect that the Allies were having to re-embark— and the men of the 'Hermann Göring' Division had proved their élite status in blood.

After the failure of this counter-attack, and with the British already making good headway up the eastern coast of the island, Guzzoni had no option but to pull his forces back to a new containment line, from which he could safely withdraw on Messina and then evacuate Sicily. There was no longer any intention to hold the island; all Guzzoni was interested in was getting as many men and as much equipment as possible safely back to the Italian mainland.

The 'Hermann Göring' Division fell back slowly, holding the US 1st and 45th Divisions in check, while on the east coast an *ad hoc* battlegroup under Schmalz tried to stem the British tide. The 15th Panzer-Grenadier Division held the west flank, and the three German units were interlinked by the dispirited Italian 'Livorno' and 'Napoli' Divisions. The 1st Fallschirmjäger Division was ordered to Sicily to reinforce this thin line, its 3rd Regiment dropping south of Catania on 12 July. It was just as well. On the 13th, the commander of the 'Napoli' Division was captured by men of the Durham Light Infantry and the division deserted en masse!

Although a sequence of British commando and airborne raids designed to break the Schmalz

Olivio–Comiso airfield complex. There was some argument as to whether it should be based in immediate support of the coastal defences, or further inland as a mobile reserve (the might of Allied aerial supremacy being acknowledged, at this time, only by those like Rommel who had experienced it at first hand). In the end, the division was assigned to cover the high ground overlooking Gela and shielding Comiso, a typical military compromise.

The Allies began swarming ashore on 10 July 1943 along two stretches of coastline: that centred on Gela, and that lying between Pachino in the south and Syracuse in the south-east. The 'Hermann Göring' Division was alerted at midnight by Sicily's Italian commander, Guzzoni.

Guzzoni was a remarkably clear-headed man who very quickly reached an appreciation of the danger points and ordered the 'Hermann Göring' Division, reinforced by the Italian 'Livorno'

Two views of the crew of a 15cm sIG.33 infantry gun on manoeuvres in Germany. Note the relatively high visibility of the white 'HG' collar patches, which explains their suppression from January 1944. (Bundesarchiv 639/4268/16 & 27)

Group's positions failed, mounting Allied pressure forced Guzzoni to maintain a steady withdrawal, pivoting on Mount Etna to what was called the 'San Stefano Line', running from the town of that name in the north-east to Catania in the south-west. The western half of Sicily was abandoned and rapidly overrun by Patton's fast-moving division. Montgomery, able to make no headway against the Fallschirmjäger units in front of Catania, now shifted the weight of his attack to the centre of the German line, the junction between the 'Hermann Göring' and 15th Panzer-Grenadier Divisions between Agira and Catenanuova. The right flank of the German line was now held by the 29th Panzer-Grenadier Division, newly arrived in Sicily.

On 26 July Mussolini resigned and was arrested 'for his own safety', which meant that the German units in Italy no longer had to serve two masters, a

Splendid shot of 'HG' gunners manning an 8.8cm flak train, possibly near Naples. Note dark blue sports shorts. (Bundesarchiv 638/4208A/26)

great military blessing. General Hube had taken command of the German units in Sicily on 15 July, and on the 27th he was ordered to prepare for immediate evacuation. Unfortunately, Montgomery attacked before he was ready, and in four days of heavy fighting succeeded in breaking the German line at Catenanuova, forcing Hube to fall back on a shorter defensive line rather prematurely. By early August the German position had become untenable, and on the 10th Hube issued evacuation orders. During the night of the 12th, 15th Panzer-Grenadier Division was shipped across the Straits of Messina, followed by the remaining German units over the next five days. By dawn on the 17th the evacuation—one of the most successful in military history—was complete. It had also taught the Germans a great deal about the art of defence when strong lines, which could only be outflanked by amphibious or airborne attacks, could be prepared across a narrow front. Four German divisions had held up more than double their own numbers for thirty-eight days—an astonishing achievement.

Interesting combinations of tropical and European service dress worn by 'HG' personnel displaying one of the priceless paintings from the Cassino collection before crating it for transport to Rome. (Bundesarchiv 729/3/30)

Italy

It was obvious to the Germans that the next Allied venture would be an amphibious landing on mainland Italy; but where? In fact, the Allies arrived at a number of alternative schemes: Operation *Musket* and *Slapstick*, aimed at Taranto; Operation *Goblet*, at Crotone; Operation *Baytown*, at Reggio; Operation *Buttress*, in the Gulf of Gioia; Operations *Giant I* and *Giant II*, airborne assaults behind the rivers Volturno and Tiber respectively; and Operation *Avalanche*, at Salerno. Against Montgomery's advice, the latter was selected. He considered Salerno too far north, and the terrain across the Sorrento Peninsula—the gateway to Naples—was difficult. But the Salerno beaches were excellent, the Americans were already talking about 'Rome by Christmas', and Allied intelligence reports misleadingly indicated the presence of only weak German units in the area. In fact, Kesselring, the brilliant commander of German forces in Italy,

had shrewdly pinpointed the Naples area as the most likely invasion point; and the 'Hermann Göring' Division, together with 15th Panzer-Grenadiers, were already in Naples refitting after the Sicilian campaign.

When Italy surrendered to the Allies on 8 September, it came as no surprise to the Germans, who had planned for just this eventuality for months. Smoothly, and with very little disturbance, Italian garrisons were disarmed and German troops moved into all the key positions. The hiatus in the Axis camp which the Allies had hoped would disrupt the German defences simply did not happen. When the American 5th Army waded ashore at Salerno on 9 September, strong German reinforcements were rapidly made available. A token holding force was left to pin Montgomery, whose 8th Army had crossed the Straits of Messina on 3 September, and all available forces were began disengaging, falling back on the first of a whole sequence of planned and prepared lines of defence running across the width of Italy.

The 'Hermann Göring' Division, in its well-entrenched positions around Sorrento, blocked the Allied advance while the harbour installations in Naples were destroyed and other German units retired behind the river Volturno. The British X Corps attacked on 23 September but could make no headway whatsoever against the stubborn Luftwaffe defenders. However, Allied attacks further inland were more successful and by the end of the month the 'Hermann Göring' Division was obliged to fall back or risk encirclement. The Germans now held a line stretching from the mouth of the river Volturno in the west to Termoli in the east, but could only field seven divisions against eleven Allied. 'Hermann Göring' Division and its comrades of the 15th Panzer-Grenadiers held the right of this line, facing the three divisions of X (British) Corps. However, the Volturno–Termoli line was purely a stop-gap measure designed to slow the Allied advance until the Todt organization had

Paul Conrath, shortly after his promotion to Generalleutnant, examines one of the Cassino manuscripts in Rome. (Bundesarchiv 729/1/32)

rushed to the Salerno area. Once again, responsibility for the defence rested with General Hube.

The brunt of the German counter-attack, spearheaded by the 'Hermann Göring' Division, fell on the more northerly British beachhead during 10–11 September, and was only deflected with difficulty. The Allies had a toe-hold in mainland Italy, but could they hang on to it? The Salerno landings had actually been made in weaker strength than those on Sicily, and without benefit of either surprise or a preliminary naval bombardment. Moreover, the Germans had the distinct advantage of occupying the high ground all around the beaches, revealing every Allied movement to their artillery observers. For several days the issue hung in doubt, as Montgomery's 8th Army slogged its way north towards Salerno; but as in Sicily, naval fire support proved decisive, and the German counter-attacks were smashed before they could make any real headway. On the 17th the Germans

Detail from a photo of trucks of the 'HG' Division carrying the Cassino treasure. This Opel 'Blitz' is camouflaged in green mottle over a dark sand-yellow ground, and carries the blue 'N' on a white disc of the division's supply battalion. Note black stencil details on door. (Bundesarchiv 729/3/16)

A group of divisional officers and NCOs in Rome. Of particular interest is the man on the left, back to camera, wearing the unique 'Meyer' tropical service cap and the rubberized motorcycle coat with field grey woollen collar. (Bundesarchiv 729/4/20)

finished its preparations along the 'Gustav Line'. By mid-October the first line had been breached in several places and the Germans fell back on their new positions, aided by heavy rain which slowed the Allied pursuit. With the onset of winter, the Allies had lost all chance of 'Rome by Christmas'.

The 'Hermann Göring' Division was now withdrawn from the front line for a well-earned rest and refit, and it was during this period that one of the best-known episodes in the division's history occurred: the rescue of the Cassino treasures. Cassino was—and is—a historic Benedictine monastery perched high on the hill which gives it its name, 1,700 feet above the Liri Valley, which was a natural 'highway to Rome' once the Allies succeeded in taking it. Monte Cassino was thus a tactical feature of no small importance but, because of its history, the 'Hermann Göring' Division was not allowed to avail itself of its dominating position. An area around the mountain was declared 'out of bounds' and clearly marked with white tape. But there was always a chance of a stray bomb or shell hitting the building, and this was what concerned

Oberstleutnant Julius Schlegel. Schlegel, a Viennese with the traditional Viennese love of the arts, was an amateur authority on Italian cultural sites, and took it on his own authority to arrange the transfer of the hundreds of paintings, sculptures, books and manuscripts from the monastery to the Vatican where, it was hoped, they would be safe. Schlegel, commander of the maintenance battalion in the 'Hermann Göring' Division, visited the monastery on 14 October and discussed his plan with the Archabbot, Dom Gregorio Diamare. The monks were initially reluctant to part with their precious treasures—there had been too many stories of Nazi looting for them to take Schlegel's offer at face value; but eventually his sincerity persuaded them, and four days later they gave their consent.

Rudolf Böhmler and Werner Haupt, in their

Crews of the 'HG' reconnaissance battalion wearing SS helmet covers with the rubberized motorcycle coat. (Bundesarchiv 639/4277/18)

book *Fallschirmjäger* (Verlag Hans-Henning Podzun, Dorheim, 1971), make the comment that 'Schlegel had assumed considerable risk by making the offer. Without knowledge of his superiors he was prepared to commit valuable motor transport, which was desperately needed for military purposes, to purely humanitarian use. He consciously violated an order which required that vehicles were to be used strictly for military transportation.' Schlegel's soldiers spent three weeks carefully packing and crating the monastery treasures, including the relic of St. Benedict himself. Then an Allied radio station announced that the men of the 'Hermann Göring' Division were looting the monastery, and Schlegel's rescue mission could no longer be kept secret. Fortunately, when he heard what had been going on, Paul Conrath gave Schlegel his full approval and official sanction to continue. The treasures were driven to Rome and handed over to a representative of the Holy See. The grateful monks conducted a special Mass for the men of the division, and presented Schlegel with an illuminated manuscript which read: 'In the name of our Lord, Jesus Christ, to the illustrious and beloved tribune, Julius Schlegel, who saved the monks and possessions of the holy monastery of Monte Cassino, these monks of Cassino give their heartfelt thanks and pray to God for his future well-being.' (Schlegel survived the war, although he lost a leg to a fighter-bomber attack in July 1944. Afterwards, the 'looting' myth persisted, and he

spent seven months in prison before no less a person than Field Marshal Alexander himself intervened and had him freed.)

Faced by the Gustav Line, the Allies meanwhile had been preparing for a new offensive. The plan they finally adopted was for a frontal assault on the Liri Valley supported by an amphibious landing behind the German lines at Anzio. The initial British assault went well, and was only checked when Kesselring threw in two reserve divisions (17 January 1944 onwards). The stubborn 15th Panzer-Grenadier Division* checked an American attack across the Rapido River, inflicting 1,700 casualties on the unlucky US 36th 'Texas' Division; but the 44th 'Hoch-und-Deutschmeister' Infantry Division fared less well against the Algerians of General Juin's French Expeditionary Corps, who broke through and made rapid progress towards Cassino. Meanwhile, on 22 January the US VI Corps landed at Anzio, behind the Gustav Line, and once again the 'Hermann Göring' Division was

*A Bavarian unit commanded by Generalmajor Eberhardt Rodt which, like the 'Hermann Göring' Division, had been virtually destroyed in Tunisia and then reformed in Sicily. It had a justifiably tough reputation.

The SdKfz 251/17 half-track, with its specially widened body to allow traverse space for the 20mm anti-aircraft cannon. The red-on-white unit insignia identifies these vehicles as belonging to 10th Light Battery, 2nd Battalion, Flak Regiment 'HG'. (Bundesarchiv 639/4276/34 & 4288/11)

called upon to try to repulse the invaders. As the Allied planners had hoped, Kesselring had committed most of his reserves to the crucial Cassino battle, and the Americans were able to wade ashore unopposed. Unhappily, their commander, General Lucas, was an unfortunate choice for the leader of a force whose only hope of success was rapid movement. Over-cautious and anxious not to offend, he allowed himself to be ruled by a 'debating society' of staff officers, and was haunted by the ghosts of Salerno. Instead of striking straight out for the Alban Hills, the key to the main road leading to Rome, he advanced slowly, building up his reserves in depth on a small beachhead, and giving Kesselring time to rush reserves to the spot.

What could have been a decisive victory was thrown away. By the time the Americans began moving away from the coast, the 'Hermann Göring' and other divisions were securely entrenched in the high ground all round.

The 'Hermann Göring' Division was stationed on the eastern sector of the front, opposite the US 3rd Division, and they faced the first American attempt to break out from the beachhead on 25 January. This attempt was stopped with ease, and the division succeeded in surrounding and capturing two US Ranger battalions during their night advance towards Cisterna. Heartened by this local success, Kesselring began planning a major offensive designed to throw the Allies back into the sea; but Alexander anticipated him and began pouring reinforcements into the beachhead. On 1 February the Anglo-American troops around the Anzio perimeter were alerted, and the German attack began during the night of the 3rd. Initially it went extremely well, and after three days' heavy fighting the British 1st Division had been thrown

The divisional insignia on the front mudguard of this SdKfz 231 '8-rad' armoured car carries the 'hand' in 10th Company position; the Viking longship appears above it. The number plates, invisible here, appeared on both rear quarters and read 'WL-45180'. The '8-rad' was probably photographed in Germany, to judge by its immaculate finish and unstowed condition. (Bundesarchiv 639/4261/35)

out of 'the Factory' (actually a workers' co-operative) and the village of Carroceto. But losses had been heavy on both sides, and the Germans were forced to regroup before continuing. On 16 February the counter-attack was renewed, with heavy assaults along the whole front, supported by a massive artillery and aerial bombardment. The 'Hermann Göring' Division was unable to make much headway against the US 3rd Division; to the north the main strike force, fourteen battalions strong and including elements of the élite 'Lehr' Division, penetrated the lines of the US 45th Division but was finally halted by the desperation of the defenders and, once more, by the devastating effects of close-range naval gunfire. The fighting continued for two more days and was rewarded by local German successes, but the first offensive had

really failed. However, the first Allied assault on Cassino had also failed after heavy losses, so honours at this point were even.

During February desultory fighting continued, and it was at this time that the 'Hermann Göring' Division was re-christened 'Hermann Göring' Fallschirmpanzerdivision. In March it was withdrawn from the line, and Goring wanted to send it to France to reform. Kesselring managed to dissuade him from this at least, and the division moved to the vicinity of Livorno, where it was out of the front line but sufficiently close to be called upon in need. The change in name did not greatly alter the division's Order of Battle. The two grenadier regiments were renamed 1st and 2nd Fallschirmgrenadierregiments, although few of their personnel had actually undergone paratroop training. However, they were reinforced from two to three battalion strength. On April 15, General Conrath was assigned to special duties and command of the division was taken over by Wilhelm Schmalz, now promoted to Generalmajor.

The division's rest was rudely interrupted on 12

May when the Allies finally broke out of the Anzio beachhead and pushed on towards Rome. Instead of being sent to France to reinforce the divisions currently preparing to repulse the imminent Operation *Overlord*, the division was thrown into the crumbling Nettuno front. Once again its arrival brought the Allied advance to a sharp halt; 'Hermann Göring' repulsed its old enemy, the US 3rd Division, near Valmonte, thus holding open the door for the escape of other German divisions trapped south of Rome. Just as things seemed to be going well for Kesselring, disaster struck. The US 36th Division, trying to outflank the German positions at Velletri, stumbled on to a tactically vital piece of high ground—the hills behind the town—and found them unoccupied. It was a mistake which was to cost the Germans dearly. The 'Hermann Göring' Division was rushed to the sector and thrown in to yet another counter-attack, but to no avail. Seizing his opportunity, General Mark Clark threw no fewer than eleven divisions against the unfortunate 'Hermann Göring' units and the 344th Infantry Division, which were forced to give way rapidly to avoid annihilation. During the night of 2–3 June they retired east of Rome, their withdrawal covered by other Luftwaffe personnel—a rearguard from 4th Fallschirmjäger Division.

On June 4 elements of the US 88th Division finally entered Rome, the prize which had been dangled before their eyes for so long and which had cost so much bloodshed. Although the German forces in Italy were far from beaten, and the 'Gothic Line' was being strengthened all the time, the heart had gone from the defence. But it was time for a change for the 'Hermann Göring' Division. On 5 July it was pulled out of the line and entrained for Germany as one of the five divisions which Hitler had promised to send General Model for his planned summer 1944 counter-offensive against the Russians.

Defeat in the East

Staging via the Brenner Pass, Rosenheim, Regensburg, Dresden, Breslau, Litzmannstadt and Skiernewice, the division finally arrived north-east of Warsaw, which had been outflanked by the Soviet 3rd Tank Corps. Playing no part in the brutal suppression of the Warsaw uprising, the division was instead assigned, along with the 19th Panzer Division and the 5th SS Panzer Division 'Wiking', to a counter-offensive against the Russian flank and rear, during which they cut the 3rd Tank Corps to pieces. Model personally congratulated the division's efforts which, he said, had 'saved Warsaw'. But it was a hollow victory, for the end was already in sight for Nazi Germany.

In August the division withdrew behind the River Vistula but, during this month and September, it continued to distinguish itself in battle against the Soviet hordes. For example, on 5 August the Sturmgeschütz company, commanded by Hauptmann Hans-Joachim Bellinger, succeeded in knocking out no fewer than thirty-six T-34s—two Russian tanks for each gun in the unit! (Bellinger received the Knight's Cross for this action, not, as recounted by Bender and Petersen, for service in Italy.)

At the beginning of October the division began a remarkable transformation into a full-fledged Panzer Korps although, like so many of Hitler's late-war innovations, the title was more impressive than the reality. Basically, the division was split

Flamethrower team in action. Note protective clothing. (Bundesarchiv 639/4273/22)

into two separate reinforced divisions, Fallschirm-panzerdivision 1 'HG' and Fallschirmpanzerdivision 2 'HG'—but each was weaker than the original parent division. They included, at last, a genuine contingent of trained paratroopers, plus two extra signal battalions and a new artillery battalion. A disadvantage of the expansion was that the bulk of the new personnel were Luftwaffe recruits with little or no ground combat training. This had the unfortunate effect of weakening the unit's overall ésprit-de-corps and fighting efficiency, although nothing can be said against the personal courage of the men. Oberst Hanns Horst von Necker was appointed commander of the 1st Division and Oberst Erich Walther of the 2nd (both men had won the Knight's Cross in Sicily and Italy). Necker was replaced in February 1945 by Oberst Max Lemke (who, as commander of a reconnaissance battalion, had also won the Knight's Cross earlier in the war).

One advantage which the two new divisions enjoyed compared with others was a centralized supply structure at Corps level, together with centralized anti-aircraft defence and a special assault battalion available as a useful mobile reserve (see diagram).

From this point onwards the unit's history is very similar to that of the 'Grossdeutschland' Panzer-Grenadier Division described in *Vanguard No. 2*. Withdrawn to East Prussia at the beginning of October 1944, it fought against the advancing Russians and even succeeded in throwing back the 11th Guard Army on 20–22 October at Nemersdorf and Angerapp; during this battle one of the division's tanks, a Panther commanded by Feldwebel Fritz Bowitz, managed single-handed to knock out thirteen Soviet tanks. For this Bowitz was awarded the Knight's Cross. Emplaced near Gumbinnen between November 1944 and January 1945, the 'Hermann Göring' Korps was involved in purely static trench warfare under the most appalling conditions—which were not improved by the Russian propaganda loudspeakers calling on the Germans to surrender. Women and food were the usual enticements!

In the middle of January 1945 the final Russian winter offensive opened with the roar of hundreds of thousands of rockets and shells. Irresistible waves of tanks and infantry ploughed forward in two spearheads aimed at Memel and Königsberg. This offensive succeeded in cutting off large numbers of German troops around Heiligenbeil, including the two 'Hermann Göring' divisions. On 25 March they were pulled out and evacuated by sea to Swinemünde and Denmark. Of the men who had formed the original Fallschirmpanzerkorps, barely a quarter survived. The remnants now fell under command of the 'Grossdeutschland' Panzerkorps, and fell or surrendered to the Russians in Saxony. Many suffered long terms of imprisonment under the Stalinist regime, and the last members of the division did not see their homes again until 1956, when the German Chancellor, Adenauer, finally made a diplomatic issue of their captivity.

The crew of an 8cm mortar setting up and serving their weapon on manoeuvres. Details of the combined Luftwaffe-SS combat uniform and the light field equipment are clearly illustrated. (Bundesarchiv 639/4260/6 & 10)

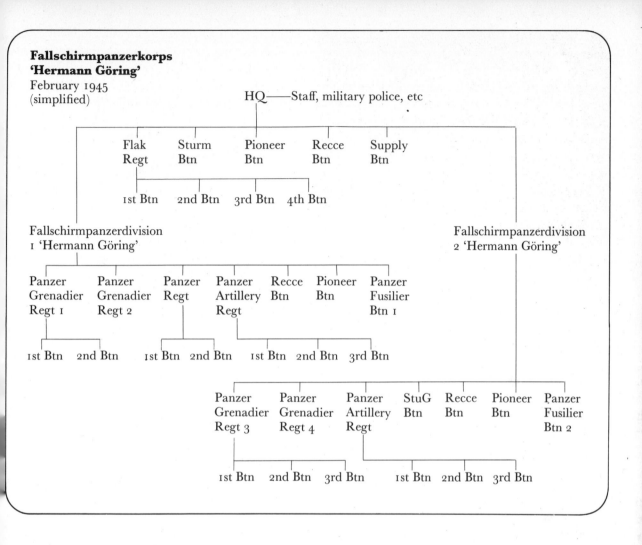

Fallschirmpanzerkorps 'Hermann Göring'
February 1945
(simplified)

HQ——Staff, military police, etc

Flak Regt | Sturm Btn | Pioneer Btn | Recce Btn | Supply Btn

1st Btn | 2nd Btn | 3rd Btn | 4th Btn

Fallschirmpanzerdivision 1 'Hermann Göring'

Panzer Grenadier Regt 1 | Panzer Grenadier Regt 2 | Panzer Regt | Panzer Artillery Regt | Recce Btn | Pioneer Btn | Panzer Fusilier Btn 1

1st Btn | 2nd Btn

1st Btn | 2nd Btn

1st Btn | 2nd Btn | 3rd Btn

Fallschirmpanzerdivision 2 'Hermann Göring'

Panzer Grenadier Regt 3 | Panzer Grenadier Regt 4 | Panzer Artillery Regt | StuG Btn | Recce Btn | Pioneer Btn | Panzer Fusilier Btn 2

1st Btn | 2nd Btn | 3rd Btn

1st Btn | 2nd Btn | 3rd Btn

Uniforms and Equipment

The original 'Hermann Göring' troops, as part of the German police force, wore police-green uniforms with light green piping down the tunic front, outside seams of the trouser legs and around the collar. Belts, straps and boots were black. Police collar patches and shoulder boards were worn, together with a special dark green cuff title introduced in December 1933 bearing in white the designation *L.P.G. General Göring*. Steel helmets bore the German red/white/black tricolour shield on the left and a white swastika, edged black, on the right.

When the regiment was transferred into the Luftwaffe, this basic uniform was retained for six months, but with the addition of a cloth Luftwaffe eagle above the right breast pocket. This eagle differed from the Army model in depicting a bird in flight to the right clutching a swastika without a wreath in its claws. Enlisted men's and NCOs' eagles were in machine-embroidered pale grey thread, officers' in silvery aluminium thread, and both appeared on dark blue-grey backing patches.

From 23 March 1936 the regiment was issued fully with Luftwaffe clothing and equipment. As time passed, however, the unit was also to acquire a variety of other clothing, including early pattern SS camouflage smocks, which will be described later.

In most respects, Luftwaffe uniform styling was very similar to that of the Army, except that it was dyed a dark blue-grey colour instead of field grey-green. Officers' headgear was the standard German

'Hermann Göring' signallers at work inside a radio car, wearing the *Fliegermütze*, the SS smock, and the *Fliegerbluse* with white collar patches. (Bundesarchiv 639/4266/4)

issue for all services, the smart peaked service cap or *Schirmmütze*; in the Luftwaffe it was of dark blue-grey material with a black ribbed band. The edges of this band and of the cap crown were piped silver, and double silver cap cords were normally worn (gold for generals). On the front of the crown was worn the Luftwaffe eagle, and on the front of the band a large and ornate badge depicting an oakleaf wreath flanked by two stylized wings, and with the red/white/black national cockade in the centre.

The most common item of headgear worn by all ranks was the Luftwaffe pattern *Feldmütze* or field cap in blue-grey material, which differed from the Army equivalent in having a tapered 'turn-up' without the scalloped front, which could not be turned down to act as protection for the ears in cold weather. Officers' field caps had silver-piped 'turn-ups' and all ranks wore the Luftwaffe eagle above the national cockade on the front. The 1943 *Einheitsfeldmütze*, or peaked field service cap for all ranks was of Army pattern with scalloped front, but of course in blue-grey material and bearing the Luftwaffe eagle. Again, officers' caps were piped silver. 'Hermann Göring' troops wore the standard German *Stalhelm* (steel helmet) in action, but painted blue-grey instead of field grey, and with a white Luftwaffe eagle decal on the left-hand side in place of the Army's black and silver eagle.

The basic issue tunic for all ranks was the *Fliegerbluse* (flight blouse), a short jacket originally designed to be worn without hindrance within the confines of an aircraft cockpit. Three basic variants existed: a tunic without hip pockets, which was originally intended to be worn by enlisted men; one with two slanting hip pockets covered by single-button flaps with rounded corners, which was originally supposed to have been worn by NCOs but which ended up being commonly worn by all ranks; and one with a pleated waist and two hip pockets without flaps, which was for officers. All featured interior pockets at breast level. The *Fliegerbluse* was usually worn open-necked, with or without the Luftwaffe pale blue shirt and black tie, but could be closed if desired by a simple hook and eye. The blouse was fastened down the front by means of four concealed soft plastic buttons, and normal collar patches and shoulder boards were worn, together with the Luftwaffe eagle on the right breast. In the 'Hermann Göring', rankers' collars were piped white, the divisional colour (in other Luftwaffe field units only officers wore collar piping, in silver).

An alternative to the *Fliegerbluse* was a more conventional, longer, single-breasted tunic with four pleated patch pockets similar in cut to the Army field service jacket but, of course, in blue-grey. This was fastened by five aluminium buttons down the front, was worn open at the neck with a shirt and tie, and had the normal collar and shoulder rank insignia. The officers' tunic was identical in cut but made of better quality material, and was normally worn as walking-out dress.

Trousers were full-cut and loose fitting, practically identical to Army issue and designed to be tucked into the long black marching boots. Officers also frequently wore flared breeches with black top-boots; generals wore broad double white stripes down the breeches' side seams. Both patterns were in blue-grey material. Apart from the marching boots, short- or tall-ankled combat boots with laces were also commonly worn in the field, while many ex-paratroops in the division succeeded in hanging on to their Fallschirmjäger jump boots, in black or brown leather. These laced across special oblique flaps designed to support the ankle on each instep, had thick rubber soles, and reached to mid-calf. Ordinary black lace-up shoes were worn by officers with walking-out dress.

Both the *Fliegerbluse* and the field service tunic could be worn with or without a belt. Officers' belts were of brown leather with an ordinary white metal buckle with two 'prongs'; enlisted men and NCOs

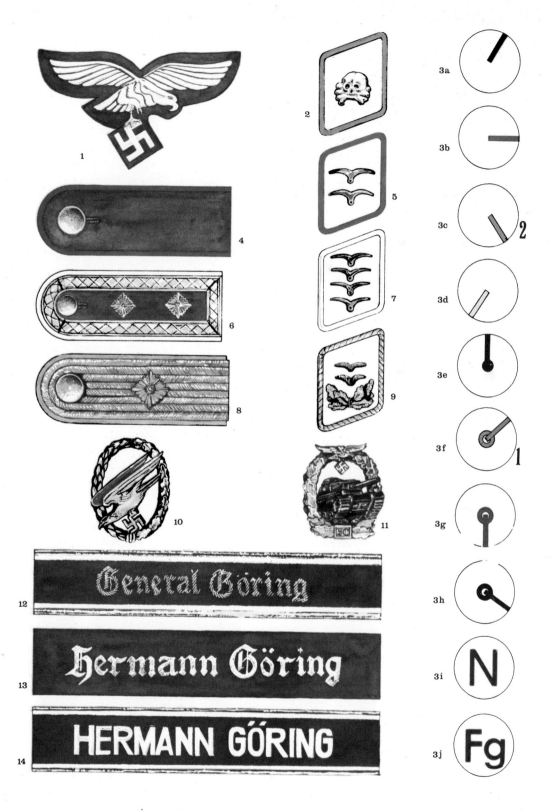

A

B   Panzer officers' Order Group, Italy, 1943

C   88mm Flak 18 gun and crew, Italy, 1943

E   Divisional personnel off duty, Italy, 1944

wore a black belt, with or without ammunition pouches, fastened by a rectangular white metal clasp (painted dull blue-grey in the field) bearing in its centre an oval oakleaf wreath surrounding an embossed Luftwaffe eagle. In the field, the standard German 'Y' strap harness could be attached to this to carry the men's equipment.

A divisional list drawn up at the beginning of 1943 summarizes the clothing and equipment issue to 'Hermann Göring' personnel: *Field dress*—steel helmet and band, forage (field) cap, *Fliegerbluse*, trousers, marching boots, greatcoat and gloves (both Luftwaffe blue-grey in colour), belt and buckle with bayonet and frog, 'Y' strap equipment harness, knapsack, gas mask and container, bread bag, canteen and cup, blanket and ground sheet. Weapons were designated as the Kar 98 carbine for enlisted men and the 9mm P.08 Luger for officers, and in addition, officers would have received leather map cases and binoculars. *Walking-out dress*—peaked uniform cap, four-pocket tunic, trousers, black shoes and Luftwaffe dress dagger. *Fatigues*—blue-grey or black twill or white denim two-piece overalls.

For tropical service there was a special Luftwaffe tropical uniform, comprising a four-pocket tunic and loose trousers with a large left thigh pocket, and tropical versions of the sidecap and field cap, all in a light sandy twill (contrasting with the Army's olive shade) and bearing the Luftwaffe cap badges, breast eagle and shoulder rank distinctions. The tropical pith helmet was also issued but appears to have been as unpopular among Luftwaffe as among Army personnel. In addition, 'Herman Göring' officers and NCOs could wear the unique Luftwaffe tropical service or 'Meyer' cap, a rather limp piece of headgear in lightweight sandy material with a large crown, a peak and a detachable neck flap designed to protect the wearer from sunstroke (which was classed as a self-inflicted wound and thus a military offence). The national and rank insignia on the band and crown were in white thread for NCOs and aluminium wire embroidery for officers. Many 'Hermann Göring' personnel, particularly in hot climates, affected brightly coloured silk scarves around their necks, although an order of 12 April 1943 prohibited their wear with walking-out dress while on leave. As in most armies, a greater degree of flexibility in dress was

An unidentified Oberst of the division wearing service tunic with full insignia. Note the early cuff-title; the details of collar and shoulder insignia; and the pilot's badge and bomber aircrew *Frontflugspange* on the left breast. (Bundesarchiv 639/4281/7)

allowed at the 'sharp end', although this never reached the outrageous extremes of the British 8th Army! In March 1944 the wearing of coloured scarves was banned completely.

In the summer of 1942 the 'Hermann Göring' Brigade began to be issued with camouflage smocks, although initially in small quantities only. These were uniformly of SS-pattern because supplies of the Army camouflage outfits were virtually non-existent at the time. SS camouflage smocks and helmet covers were made, as were the Army's, in reversible material designed to allow their wearers to blend in with natural conditions at particular times of year. Whereas the Army smocks were merely 'two-tone'—winter white and summer splinter pattern—the SS versions were available in spring-summer-autumn-winter colours. The winter smock was white, of course, with either an

Oberleutnant Karl Rossman, commander of the 1st Battalion, Panzer Regiment 'HG', in an SdKfz 250 or 251 radio command half-track; he wears a camouflaged helmet, the black Panzer vehicle uniform with white-piped collar patches, silver or white collar piping, and the Knight's Cross he won in Russia in 1941. (Bundesarchiv 639/4288/23)

autumn or a spring reverse. From spring to autumn the following basic colours were used: spring (1)—beige, pink, white, dark and light green; spring (2)—stone, beige, pink, dark and light green; summer (1)—light, medium and dark green; summer (2)—four shades of green; summer (3)—beige and four shades of green; autumn (1)—khaki, rust and dark green; autumn (2)—stone, beige, rust and dark green; and autumn (3)—beige-pink, rust, brown and dark green. Some of these patterns, which were theoretically a good idea, but which must have made storekeeping a nightmare, are illustrated in the colour plates.

The basic SS smock was a 'pullover', eyeholed at the neck to be closed with drawstrings. It had no collar; elasticated or buttoned wrists; and elasti-

cated or drawstringed waist. Slits in the upper half of the smock enabled the wearer to reach pockets in his tunic underneath, and later patterns also embodied a pair of breast pockets with flaps and/or numerous cloth loops on shoulders, arms, chest, etc, into which foliage could be tucked for additional concealment. A later-pattern camouflage jacket with four pockets was also produced, but it is unclear whether this was ever issued to the 'Hermann Göring' Division.

The two Fallschirmjäger battalions incorporated into the 'Hermann Göring' Brigade and sent to Tunisia were issued with German paratroop-pattern thigh-length splinter camouflage jump smocks, and a later variation of these was also seen in East Prussia towards the end of the war, but never in large quantities. Similarly, during the winter of 1944–5 in the latter theatre,

'Hermann Göring' grenadiers from 1st Company, 2nd Battalion, riding in SdKfz 15 trucks. Again, note the high visibility of the white collar patches. (Bundesarchiv 639/4260/33A)

the division received an issue of the warm, reversible mouse grey/white Army two-piece snow-suits, but on what scale is unknown. For most of the war the SS-pattern smocks remained standard within the division, and were worn by Panzer and self-propelled gun crews as well as ground troops.

Tank crewmen within the division wore the normal army double-breasted short black Panzer jacket and loose trousers, with the Luftwaffe eagle on the right breast and white or silver collar piping. Self-propelled gun crews received uniforms of the same cut, but in either army field-grey or Luftwaffe blue-grey instead of black. A wide variety of mixed uniform styles can be seen in the photographs, including camouflage smocks over black Panzer trousers and black Panzer jackets over blue-grey Luftwaffe trousers etc.

But if the 'Hermann Göring' Division's personnel wore a confused mixture of Luftwaffe, Army and SS clothing, three items still distinguished them immediately from all other German field units: their collar patches, shoulderstraps and cuffbands.

The following general description of insignia should be read with this chronological sequence firmly in mind: From October 1937 the 'HG' Regiment wore white collar patches* edged green, except for flak personnel who had red edging, and paratroops who had yellow edging. All wore white *Waffenfarbe* on the shoulderstraps. From January 1943 to April 1943 all branches wore individual *Waffenfarbe* edging on collar patches, but kept white shoulderstrap *Waffenfarbe*. After April 1943 collar patches lost their coloured edging, and branch *Waffenfarbe* was worn on shoulderstraps. For visibility reasons white collar patches were ordered abandoned in the field from January 1944, metal ranking being applied directly to collars.

The basic shape of the collar patches was a lozenge, squarer in shape than the Army pattern, and with rounded corners, like those of the SS. On these patches were stylized eagles and oakleaf wreaths denoting rank. A private (i.e. grenadier,

*Administration, ordnance and medical personnel wore dark green, bright red or dark blue respectively.

jäger, pioneer, gunner, driver, etc) wore a white lozenge collar patch with a single silver-grey (aluminium) 'eagle' in the centre, and *Waffenfarbe* edging. His shoulderstraps were blue-grey with *Waffenfarbe* edging. A Gefreiter had two eagles on his collar patch and, in addition, a single chevron, point down, on his upper left arm. An Obergefreiter had three eagles on his collar patch and two chevrons on his arm, while a Hauptgefreiter or Stabsgefreiter had four eagles and three chevrons (from 1944 two chevrons and a 'pip'). An Unteroffizier reverted to one eagle on his collar patch, but his shoulderstraps were outlined in silver-grey *Tresse* (lace) on the long sides and inner end. An Unterfeldwebel had two eagles and his shoulderstraps laced round the whole edge. A Feldwebel had three eagles, and a pip in the centre of his shoulderstraps; an Oberfeldwebel four eagles and two pips; and a Stabsfeldwebel four eagles and

Unidentified officers of the division displaying to advantage the Luftwaffe service tunic and 'flyer's blouse'. Left, a Hauptmann in the simplified service tunic with straight pocket flaps; right, an Oberleutnant in the *Fliegerbluse*, wearing the Iron Cross 1st Class, the ribbon of the 2nd Class, and the General Assault Badge. (Bundesarchiv 639/4278/33)

three pips. Unteroffiziers and up wore *Tresse*-edged collars, also.

Officers' collar patches were edged with silver cord and ran in the same sequence, with one, two or three eagles for a Leutnant (2nd Lieutenant), Oberleutnant (Lieutenant) or Hauptmann (Captain), above an oakleaf spray. Their shoulderstraps were made of lines of silver-grey cord on a *Waffenfarbe* backing, with two (Hauptmann), one (Oberleutnant) or no pips (Leutnant) respectively. Field officers also had one (Major), two (Oberstleutnant—Lieutenant-Colonel) or three (Oberst—Colonel) collar patch eagles, but surrounded by a complete oakleaf wreath, while their shoulderstraps appeared as interwoven silver-grey cords with no (Major), one (Oberstleutnant) or two (Oberst) gold pips. A Generalmajor's (Major-General's) shoulder insignia was similar to that of a Major but in mixed gold and silver triple cord;

while that of a Generalleutnant (Lieutenant-General, and the highest rank ever achieved by a serving 'Hermann Göring' officer) was the same with a silver shoulder pip. Collar patch insignia for these ranks were one and two eagles respectively, in complete wreaths; the insignia and cord patch edging were gold.

Arm of service or *Waffenfarbe* colours, usually to the army pattern, were used to edge the collar patches and shoulderstraps as follows: white for infantry (grenadiers), pink for Panzer troops, red for artillery and flak personnel, golden- and lemon-yellow respectively for reconnaissance and signal troops, black for pioneers, light blue for supply and workshop troops, dark blue for medical personnel, orange for military policemen (Feldgendarmerie), dark green striped with lemon yellow for field post troops and violet for chaplains.

Rank and speciality were thus easily identified, but members of the 'Hermann Göring' Division also wore cuff titles. As noted earlier, the first of these was the white-on-green Landespolizeigruppe cuffband. This was replaced in March 1936 by a silver-grey on dark blue *'General Göring'* title

General Conrath, accompanied by Lt. Musil of the Panzer Pionier Kompanie, inspects 'Hermann Göring' recruits at Berlin-Reinickendorf. The enlisted men's *Fliegerbluse* is shown clearly. (Bundesarchiv 639/4292/29)

which, although officially superseded by other variants, continued to be worn throughout the war as shown in many of the accompanying photographs. In May 1942 a new Gothic script title '*Hermann Göring*' was officially introduced, but shortly afterwards this was replaced by a band with the same name in block capitals. Both were edged with silver braid for officers, and without edging for other ranks. The '*General Göring*' title could still be seen being worn (by none other than the divisional commander among others) as late as the end of 1943 and by other ranks until the end of the war, as illustrated. This is a prime example of the discrepancies between orders and actual practice, which appear to befuddle many amateur military historians!

All these cuffbands were 33mm wide and were supposed to be worn 16cm above the bottom of the right sleeve on all uniform jackets, excluding fatigues and camouflage smocks. However, it is apparent that many 'Hermann Göring' personnel went without cuffbands at times, as large numbers of the division's troops can be seen without them in

Excellent photograph of a Gefreiter of the division in Italy, his rank patches clearly visible on the collar of the blouse turned down over the SS smock; he holds the standard Kar 98 rifle fitted with a grenade-throwing adaptor. (Bundesarchiv 639/4263/14)

numerous photographs. Men entitled to wear them could also be seen with '*Kreta*' or '*Afrika*' cuffbands on their lower left sleeves.

Vehicle identification markings

The 'Hermann Göring' Division utilized a remarkably logical device on its vehicles and guns which not only identified the division, but also the arm of service and individual company all in one: a white circle with a bar, like the hand of a clock, in different colours. The position of the 'hand' on the 'dial' indicated the company number, and its colour the arm of service. Where two regiments existed (ie, the two grenadier regiments), the 1st Regiment's dial had a small inner circle in the same colour as the hand while, in addition, the number of the regiment was painted in black Arabic numerals alongside the four o'clock position. In some cases,

Roman numerals alongside the eight o'clock position were used to denote the battalion within a regiment. The arm of service colours used for the hands were as follows: green for grenadiers, red for flak and artillery units, black for Panzer and pioneer (engineer) units and yellow for reconnaissance units. To differentiate between the flak and artillery regiments, and between the Panzer and pioneer battalions, the latter units also had a small inner ring in the appropriate colour. A glance at the first colour plate will illustrate these points.

Some units carried a blue letter denoting their arm of service instead of the hand, including 'N' for supply troops, 'S' for medical units and 'Fg' for military police.

In the field, these markings were repeated on divisional signposts by the roadside. These signposts were painted in the arm of service colour for regimental headquarters, in white for 1st Battalion HQ, in red for the 2nd, yellow for the 3rd and blue for the 4th. In addition, the unit commander's name appeared in black capital letters alongside the 'dial'.

When the division was expanded into a corps in 1944 a revised system of vehicle markings was

Men of the 'Hermann Göring' Brigade photographed during the later stages of the Tunisian fighting, spring 1943. (Bundesarchiv 730/106/10)

required, although there appears to be little photographic evidence that the new system was ever widely implemented. The 1st Division retained its original 'dial' system, while the 2nd Division based their insignia on the same 'clock hand' principle but on a diamond-shaped white background. Corps troops used the white 'dial' with appropriate arm of service pointer, the whole within a red diamond, edged black.

Vehicles and weapons

The German ground forces used such a variety of tanks, guns, trucks, half-tracks and other assorted vehicles and weapons that it would be impossible to describe them all here. The following comments are thus restricted to those most commonly used by the division. It seems appropriate to begin with the flak artillery.

The most commonplace German anti-aircraft gun was the 20mm Flak 38, a Mauser design with an effective cyclic rate of around 200rpm firing a 0.2625lb shell to a ceiling of slightly over 6,600 feet. This weapon and the earlier, slower-firing Flak 30, equipped the majority of the light flak batteries and was especially useful against low-flying ground attack aircraft. It could also be used against 'soft' ground targets with devastating effect. When grouped in fours on a single mounting as the

quadruple Flakvierling 38 this gun became one of the most feared of all anti-aircraft weapons encountered by low-flying Allied aircrews. The basic gun was fitted with two wheels and could be towed behind any sort of light or medium truck, but as the war progressed both the single and quadruple mounts were fitted on half- and full-tracked chassis such as the SdKfz 251, SdKfz 7 and PzKpfw IV as self-propelled guns, especially in the Panzer and Panzer-Grenadier divisions. The Flak 38 could also fire an AP 40 armour-piercing round, although it was never classified as an anti-tank weapon.

Firing a heavier (1.4lb) shell to an effective ceiling of over 11,500 feet were the 3.7cm Flak 18, 36, 37 and 43 guns, which were also issued to light flak batteries. All used the same ammunition but had different cyclic rates of fire varying from 80 to 180rpm. This gun was also mounted on a variety of self-propelled chassis, and was produced in limited numbers in double-barrelled form as the 3.7cm Flakzwilling 43.

Bypassing the 5cm and 7.5cm weapons, which were never particularly successful and were only used in small quantities by coastal and other reserve units, one comes to the notorious '88', the Krupp-designed 8.8cm Flak 18 and its derivatives, the Flak 36, 37 and 41. Unquestionably one of the best designed guns of all time, the '88' required a detachment of commander and nine men, and could hurl its 20 to 21lb shells to heights of 26,000 to 49,000 feet at a rate of 15 to 20rpm. It also proved that it could act very effectively in the anti-tank role; the basic Flak 18/36/37 was able to penetrate up to nearly four inches (100mm) of armour plate at 2,000 yards' range and its successors, which were designed especially for this task, over six inches (150mm) at 2,500 yards. Variants of this gun were mounted on SP chassis as tank-destroyers, and it formed the main armament of the PzKpfw VI Tiger I and Tiger II tanks.

Heavier flak guns in the Luftwaffe's inventory included the little-known 10.5cm Flak 38 and Flak 39, firing 33lb shells to a height of 42,000 feet; and the 12.8cm Flak 40 which fired a 57lb shell to 48,500 feet. Both these weapons were too heavy for normal field use and were usually found in static emplacements or on railway mountings. A version of the 12.8 was, however, fitted to the monstrous Jagdtiger, though none of these unwieldy—but

Luftwaffe recruits receiving basic small arms training. They wear the white denim fatigues, which proved highly impractical. In the foreground is the MG 15 light machine-gun. (Bundesarchiv 638/4204/10)

powerful—tank destroyers found their way into the 'Hermann Göring' Division's hands.

German artillery regiments principally utilized guns of two calibres, both of which are still in widespread use today: 10.5 and 15cm. Artillery companies in infantry regiments were issued with smaller 7.5cm weapons, while heavy artillery batteries usually had a quota of 17 and/or 21cm weapons. The most common 7.5cm weapon was the leIG 18, a Rheinmetall design of antiquated appearance but with the useful ability to hurl a 6.6lb shell nearly 4,000 yards. The superior Krupp Feldkanone 18 with its longer barrel was able to fire a shell twice this weight over 10,000 yards, but was actually more expensive to produce than the 10.5cm leFH 18 and thus saw more limited action. The latter gun was the backbone of the German field artillery and superior to the British 25 pdr. Designed by Rheinmetall again, it was a rugged and very sound weapon capable of firing its 32.65lb shells to a range of over 11,500 yards. A hybrid version, with the original barrel mounted on the lighter Pak 40 anti-tank gun carriage, was also produced in an attempt to improve the weapon's

mobility, but the carriage was too light and this was never a real success.

Of all the German infantry guns produced, by far the most powerful was the 15cm sIG 33, which could fire a variety of ammunition types, including a useful stick bomb which was employed in clearing barbed wire entanglements. The basic HE shell weight was just under 84lb and maximum range just over 5,000 yards. Although of the same calibre, 15cm, the sFH 18 was classified as a heavy rather than an infantry or field gun, but was a more effective weapon. Its split trail carriage enhanced its performance, and its much longer barrel could take a 96lb shell and throw it to a maximum range of 14,600 yards.

Other 15cm weapons deployed included the rather inaccurate sFH 18/40 and the enormously long-barrelled Kanone 18 which had a range of nearly 27,000 yards. More popular—when available, because demand always exceeded supply—was the 17cm K18, an excellent heavy artillery piece which also found favour with American and British troops when they succeeded in capturing one. Despite its size, this Krupp weapon could be deployed rapidly and fired a 138lb shell over 32,000 yards. It had originally been designed to replace the heavier 21cm Mrs 18, but this large and versatile weapon remained in use throughout the war, firing a 285lb shell to over 18,000 yards range. Many 10.5 and 15cm artillery pieces were eventually mounted on a variety of armoured SP chassis, mainly of obsolete or captured designs but including the PzKpfw IV.

In addition to the '88', the Wehrmacht—including the 'Hermann Göring' Division—used several other anti-tank guns, foremost amongst which was the 7.5cm Pak 40, another Rheinmetall design. Light, and with a very low carriage, this superb weapon fired a 7lb shell at a muzzle velocity of 3,060fps, giving it an armour penetration ability of $4\frac{1}{2}$ inches (115mm) at 500 yards (30° obliquity). A variant of this weapon was installed in the PzKpfw V Panther tank, while the basic design was also mounted in a variety of half- and full-tracked

SP chassis as a tank destroyer, and in the larger eight-wheeled German armoured cars.

The subject of German tanks has been covered so thoroughly elsewhere, and the number of marks and variants is so long that it would be foolhardy to attempt a full listing here. Those used principally by the 'Hermann Göring' Division, however, were the PzKpfw III, PzKpfw IV and Panther.

The vehicle which became the PzKpfw III was originally intended to provide the mainstay of the German armoured forces, but experience in the early Polish and French campaigns led to the rapid dismissal of this idea for, although superior in many respects to most other contemporary designs, it lacked armour protection and 'punch'. Its frontal armour was a mere 15mm, although this was later increased to 30 and then 50mm; and its main armament in the initial stages was the little 3.7cm. Fortunately Daimler-Benz, the designers, had allowed a generous turret ring, allowing heavier calibre weapons to be fitted. These eventually included the long-barrelled 5cm anti-tank gun and a 7.5cm infantry support weapon. The most successful variant of this tank, used by the 'Hermann Göring' Division, was the Ausf M, which weighed 22 tons, had a top speed of 25mph, a range of 108 miles, 50mm frontal armour, and mounted the 5cm L/60 gun which could penetrate $2\frac{1}{8}$ inches (54mm) of armour plate at nearly 900 yards' range.

Similar in general appearance to the PzKpfw III, the Krupp-designed PzKpfw IV was a much sounder vehicle and provided the backbone of the Panzer divisions throughout the war. Like the PzKpfw III it was produced in a variety of versions, progressively up-armoured and up-gunned, and was eventually manufactured in greater quantities than any other German tank. The most successful variants were those equipped with long-barrelled 7.5cm guns—the Ausf F2, G, H and J. Although longer, wider, higher and more heavily armed than the PzKpfw III, it weighed little more and had a similar turn of speed, while its range, utilizing the detachable external fuel tank on the hull rear, was far greater at 186 miles. Its frontal armour was comparable but rose to an eventual 80mm with appliqué plates, while hull and turret 'skirts' improved its survival qualities against hollow-charge projectiles. Its L/48 7.5cm gun was not as good as the L/70 fitted to the Panther, but could

Generalmajor Schmalz, commander of the 'Hermann Göring' from 16 April 1944 until the end of the war (left, in sheepskin coat) presenting the Knight's Cross to divisional personnel in East Prussia after heavy fighting against the Russians. Recipients are, from left to right: Uffz. Werner Grunhold, Gfr. Konrad Steets, Gfr. Albert Plapper, and an unidentified Panzer commander (note skull motif pinned directly to collar) who may be Fritz Bowitz. (Bundesarchiv 77/93/6)

still penetrate 3½ inches (90mm) of armour plate at its effective range of 900 yards.

The PzKpfw V Panther is normally considered the best German tank design of the war, even though it was a 'copy' of the Soviet T-34. Hurriedly planned after the invasion of Russia in 1941 had shown up the inadequacies of the PzKpfw III and IV, its best features were its thick and well-sloped armour plates and its excellent 7.5cm L/70 cannon. It entered service in Russia in the summer of 1943 and served on to the end of the war. Indeed, a few old Panthers have been observed in Arab service during post-war tank battles in the Middle East! Carrying a crew of five men, and weighing-in at 45 tons, it had a top speed of nearly 29mph and a range of 55 miles. Its bow armour was 80mm thick (turret 120mm) and its 7.5cm gun was capable of

penetrating four inches (102mm) at 1,000 yards' range.

Other full-tracked armoured fighting vehicles used by the 'Hermann Göring' Division included the StuG III, an assault gun mounting a 7.5cm weapon in a non-traversing superstructure on the PzKpfw III chassis; the Marder II and III, tank destroyers mounting either the 7.5cm Pak 40 or captured Russian 76.2mm guns on obsolete PzKpfw II and PzKpfw 38(t) chassis; and various SP artillery pieces such as the 10.5cm Wespe and 15cm Hummel.

The Plates

Badges and Insignia

A1 Luftwaffe eagle
This basic design was worn on the right breast of all Luftwaffe tunics and blouses, on the upper front surface of all caps, in a wreath on the enlisted men's belt buckle plate, and in reversed form on the left side of steel helmets, as a decal.

A2 Panzer uniform collar patch
One of several variants; the pink *Waffenfarbe* piping was only authorized between January and April 1943. Elongated black patches of Army design but with white piping were the original insignia, and many remained in use after the white patch officially replaced them. The final style was to wear the skull pinned directly to the collar without a patch. Former Army personnel often retained the long black patches piped in pink.

A3 Vehicle identification markings
(a) 1st Coy., 1st Bn., Panzer Rgt. 'HG' (b) 3rd Coy., Ist Bn., Flak Rgt. 'HG' (c) 5th Coy., 2nd Bn., 2nd Grenadier Rgt. 'HG' (d) 7th Coy., Reconnaissance Bn. 'HG' (e) HQ Coy., Panzer Rgt. 'HG' (f) 2nd Coy., 1st Bn., Ist Grenadier Rgt. 'HG' (g) 6th Coy., Artillery Rgt. 'HG' (h) 4th (Bridging) Coy., Pz. Pioneer Bn. 'HG' (i) Supply Bn. (j) Military Police unit

General Conrath (right) with an unidentified Oberst, somewhere in Italy; in the background, PzKpfw III tanks and Panzer personnel of the division. (Bundesarchiv 639/4283/12)

A4, A5 Gefreiter shoulderstrap and collar patch
The red piping indicates the Flak or Artillery regiments. See p. 29 for dates of regulation changes.

A6, A7 Oberfeldwebel shoulderstrap and collar patch
The white piping indicates one of the Grenadier regiments (see also p. 29).

A8, A9 Oberleutnant shoulderstrap and collar patch
The yellow underlay indicates the Reconnaissance battalion (see also p. 29).

A10 Parachutist badge
Instituted in November 1936, this badge was worn on the lower left breast by all qualified parachutists.

A11 Luftwaffe Tank Combat Badge
Instituted in November 1944, this badge existed in two variants. The basic award, for three separate engagements on three separate days, lacked the small cartouche of the higher grade badge illustrated; this denoted service in 25, 50, or 75

37

combats. It was awarded to Panzer, Panzer-Grenadier, armoured reconnaissance, and other personnel who served in armoured vehicles.

A12 'General Göring' Regiment cuffband
Instituted in March 1936 for wear by all ranks of the regiment; lettering was in grey for enlisted ranks, with piped edges for NCOs, and in silver with silver-piped edges for officers.

A13 'Hermann Göring' Division transitional cuffband
Replaced the regimental cuffband in May 1942—although the early pattern was still widely observed—and was itself replaced after a matter of months by A14.

A14 'Hermann Göring' Division cuffband, final version
Officer's version—enlisted ranks wore a band with similar block lettering in light grey, without piped edges.

B Panzer Officers' Orders Group, Italy, 1943
On the left is a despatch rider with a BMW R75/A1 motorcycle—note reconnaissance unit insignia on mudguard beneath number plate. The rider wears an improvised hot-weather motoring overall—the Luftwaffe's lightweight canvas flying suit, noticeable in photographs of 'HG' motorcyclists and incorrectly identified elsewhere as a purpose-built motorcycle suit. On the left of the central group is a Hauptmann of the Panzer Regiment 'HG', in black vehicle uniform with collar patches in the division's white *Waffenfarbe*, shoulderstrap underlay in Panzer pink *Waffenfarbe*, and an officer's-pattern cuffband. Next to him is an elegant Panzer Regiment Leutnant, wearing a combination of uniform items which was strictly unofficial but which is confirmed by photographs—the Luftwaffe *Schirmmütze* and breeches, with the black Panzer jacket. He wears the Army-pattern collar patches with 'HG' white piping. In the right foreground is another Panzer officer wearing the SS camouflage smock and helmet cover in summer pattern colours, over his black Panzer uniform. On the right is a Leutnant of the self-propelled artillery element, in the rare (but confirmed) Luftwaffe-blue version of the SP artillery vehicle uniform, complete with 1943 *Einheitsmütze* piped silver for commissioned rank. The skulls from the collar-patches are pinned

directly to the collar, a common practice in 1944–45. In the background is a PzKpfw IIIL tank with long-barrelled 5cm gun, in the standard overall sand yellow camouflage paint, with turret numbers and tactical sign of HQ Company, 2nd Bn., Panzer Rgt. 'HG'.

C 88mm Flak 18 gun and crew, Italy, 1943–44
An 88mm Flak 18 engaging a ground target with high explosive ammunition (*Sprengranate Patrone L/4.5*). In the summer heat most of the crew are in various stages of casual undress; some wear the Luftwaffe tropical uniform, some the blue shorts of the issue sports kit, some blue-grey helmets and some sand-painted tropical style helmets. The officer, a Leutnant of the Flak Rgt. 'HG', wears the standard Luftwaffe tropical uniform tunic and trousers, with the 'Meyer' cap. Colourful scarves were a popular affectation in the division. The tactical sign of the 2nd (Heavy) Bty. is painted on a mudguard of the detachable two-bogie gun carriage.

D Light flak in action, Italy, 1943–44
Allied air superiority in the Mediterranean theatre was often a decisive factor, although the German forces became, of necessity, adept at moving troops and vehicles under cover of night or bad weather. These conditions forced Germany to develop a wide range of mobile anti-aircraft vehicles, particularly for protection against low-flying Allied fighter-bombers. Two of these are shown here in action. The SdKfz 10/4, a light unarmoured half-track mounting a single Flak 38 weapon of 20mm calibre, is shown on the left. The crew wear SS-pattern camouflage smocks over the standard blue Luftwaffe service uniform. On the right is an SdKfz 251/17, a variant of the ubiquitous 'Hanomag', built specially to Luftwaffe specifications and also mounting a Flak 38; the sides of the rear compartment folded out and down in action. Both are marked with the insignia of the division's 10th (Light) Flak Battery. Photographs show the division's SdKfz 251/17 crews wearing black Panzer vehicle uniform with, presumably, red *Waffenfarbe* on the shoulderstraps. (A Flak 38 is preserved in the Imperial War Museum collection at Duxford, near Cambridge.)

Combinations of Luftwaffe, Panzer and SS clothing worn by officers and men of the armoured elements in Italy; the vehicle is an SdKfz 16 radio car. (Bundesarchiv 639/4277/6)

E Divisional personnel off duty, Italy, 1944

A peaceful game of 'skat' in an Italian bar. On the left is an Unteroffizier wearing the popular *Fliegerbluse* with the white *Waffenfarbe* of one of the Grenadier regiments; the enlisted men's version of the divisional cuffband is illustrated here. From January 1944 onwards the white collar patches were abandoned and the ranking 'wings' were pinned directly to the collar; the silver NCO *Tresse* was replaced by grey lace. Centre is an Unterfeldwebel in the four-pocket Luftwaffe service tunic, worn as walking-out dress with the NCO's peaked cap, and straight trousers worn over black laced shoes. The yellow *Waffenfarbe* and specialist arm badge identify an NCO of a signals unit. On the right is a Gefreiter in the Luftwaffe's standard tropical uniform, which carried no collar patches or collar piping. His shoulderstraps identify him as a Grenadier; his parachutist badge, and the old-style cuffband retained despite regulations, indicate a former member of one of the parachute units drafted into the division at an early date.

Farbtafeln

A Abzeichen

A1 Das Adlerabzeichen der Luftwaffe auf Mützen und Waffenröcken getragen und auf Stahlhelmen umgekehrt.

A2 Panzerabzeichen für Kragen, eine mehrerer Arten, die in den letzten Jahren der Kriegszeit tatsächlich zusammengetragen wurden. Andere waren weiss ohne den Schnurbesatz; und schwarz mit weissem Schnurbesatz. Der Kopf wurde später gerade auf den Kragen geheftet.

A3 *Fahrzeugskennzeichen*: (a) 1ste Komp., Panzerrgt. (b) 3te Komp., 1ste Abt., Flakrgt., (c) 5ten Komp., 2ten Abt., 2ten Grenadierrgt. (d) 7ten Komp., Streifeabt. (e) Hauptquartier Komp., Panzerrgt. (f) 2ten Komp., 1ste Abt., Grenadierrgt. (g) 6ten Komp., Artilleriergt. (h) 4ten Brücken-Baukompanie, Panzer Pionier Abt., (i) Nachschubkomp., (j) Feldgendarmerie.

A4, A5 Achselstück und Kragenabzeichen, Gefreiters, Flak oder Artillerie.

A6, A7 Achselstück und Kragenabzeichen, Oberfeldwebels, Grenadiers.

A8, A9 Achselstück und Kragenabzeichen, Oberleutnants, Streifeverband.

A10 Abzeichen Fallschirmjägers.

A11 Panzerkampfabzeichen der Luftwaffe. Eingeführt in November 1944 hatte dies grundlegendes Muster keine kleine Kartusche unten, wie man hier illustriert hat; diese zeigte Nummer Kampfhandlungen—25, 50 und 75.

A12 Regimentsarmbinde 'General Göring' von März 1936 getragen. Truppen trugen Armbinden mit grauer Bezeichnung mit Buchstaben. Armbinden Uffzs mit grauer Bezeichnung mit Buchstaben und grauen Schnurbesatz. Armbinde Offiziere mit silberer Bezeichnung mit Buchstaben und silberen Schnurbesatz. Diese Armbinde wurde gelegentlich noch spät in dem Krieg benutzt.

A13 Divisionsarmbinde 'Hermann Göring' für eine kleine Zeit von Mai 1942 getragen.

A14 Divisionsarmbinde 'Hermann Göring', die nach ein paar Monate das frühere Modell ersass. Truppen trugen hellgraue Bezeichnung mit Buchstaben. Offizier trugen silbere Bezeichnung mit Buchstaben und silberen Schnurbesatz.

B Unterredung Panzeroffiziere, Italien, 1943

Meldefahrer trägt Fluganzug der Luftwaffe als Autofahrenarbeitsanzug; Krad BMW R75/A1 hat Streifeverbandsabzeichen auf Kotflügel. Zur Linken der Gruppe ist ein Hauptmann auf schwarzer Panzeruniform mit Feldmütze, Armbinde mit Offiziersmuster, weisse Kragenabzeichen und Achselstück mit rosa Schnurbesatz versehen. Daneben ihn ist ein feiner Leutnant, der teilweise blaue Dienstuniform der Luftwaffe und teilweise schwarze Panzeruniform, mit schwarzen Kragenabzeichen mit weissem Schnurbesatz versehen trägt. Der dritte Offiziere trägt Tarnungskleidung des SS-Musters über seiner schwarzen Panzeruniform. Der Vierter, ein Leutnant des Selbstfahrartellerieverbands, trägt eine Luftwaffe-blaue Sonderversion dieser Kommissuniform die Waffengattung und die Mütze mit Schirm 1943s mit silberem Schnurbesatz. Bemerken Kopfabzeichen gerade auf den Kragen geheftet. Der Panzer is das PzKpfw III mit Bezeichnungen Hauptquartierskompanie, 2ten Bataillon, Panzer Rgt. 'HQ'.

C Flakgewehr 18 18mm, Italien 1943

In der Sommerwärme sind die Bedienung teilweise auf Tropenuniform der Luftwaffe-ausstattung teilweise auf Sportkleidungen bekleidet. Der Offizier trägt die 'Meyer' Mütze und Kommisskleidung mit dem roten Schnurbesatz des Flakregiments. Die Abzeichen der 2ten (schweren) Batterie wird auf der Lafette angestricht. Die Granaten sind Sprengranate Patronen L/4.5.

D Leichtflak im Gefecht, Italien, 1943–44

Zur Links ist eine Halbkette SdKfz 10/4, die eine Flakkanone 38 30mm in Stellung bringt; die Bedienung trägt Tarnungskleidungen SS-Musters über blauen Luftwaffeuniformen. Zur Rechten ist eine Halbkette SdKfz 251/7, die auch die Flak 38 in Stellung bringt, mit Bedienung auf schwarzen Panzeruniformen bekleidet. Die Abzeichen auf den Fahrzeugen identifizieren die Divisione 10ten (Leichte) Flakbatterie.

E Divisionsmannschaften, Italien, 1944–45

Drei Soldaten geniessen ein Spiel 'Skat' in einem italienischen Café. Zur Links ein Unteroffizier auf allgemein getragenen Fliegerbluse, sein weisser Schnurbesatz identifiziert einen Grenadierverband. Von Januar 1944 wurden die weisse Kragenabzeichen durch die 'Fliegerabzeichen' aus Metall gerade auf den Kragen geheftet ersetzen und die silbere Spitze Uffzs wurde durch graue Spitze ersetzen. In der Mitte. ein Unterfeldwebel auf Fusskleidung, die aus dem Dienstwaffenrock der Luftwaffe mit vier Taschen, Mütze mit Schirm und Hosen besteht. Die gelbe Waffenfarbe und das Armdienstabzeichen identifizieren einen Signalverband. Seine Armbinde frühen Musters und Dienstabzeichen Fallschirmjägers identifiziert ihn als ein der Fallschirmjäger früh in dem Divisionslaufbahn dazu ernannt.

Notes sur les planches en couleur

A Insignes

A1 L'écusson d'aigle de Luftwaffe porté sur chapeaux et tuniques, et, renversé sur casques d'acier.

A2 Insignes du col de Panzer, un de plusieurs styles qui dans la pratique furent portés ensemble dans la dernière période de la guerre. Autres furent blancs sans le tuyautage; et noirs avec tuyautage blanc. Le 'crâne' fut vu plus tard epinglé directement au col.

A3 Marquages d'identification de véhicules: (a) 1ère Compagnie, 1er Bataillon, Rgt. Panzer. (b) 3ème Compagnie, 1er Bataillon, Rgt. Flak. (c) 5ème Compagnie, 2ème Bataillon, 2ème Rgt. Grenadier. (d) 7ème Compagnie, Bataillon de Reconnaissance (e) Compagnie générale, Rgt. Panzer (f) 2ème Compagnie, 1er Bataillon, 1er Rgt. Grenadier (g) 6ème Compagnie, Régiment d'Artillerie (h) 4ème Compagnie Pontoniere, Bataillon Panzer Pionier (i) Bataillon d'intendance (j) Détachment de Gendarmerie.

A4, A5 Patte d'épaule et insignes du col, Gefreiter, Flak ou Artillerie.

A6, A7 Patte d'épaule, et insignes du col, Oberfeldwebel, Grenadiers.

A8, A9 Patte d'épaule et insignes du col, Oberleutnant, bataillon de reconnaissance.

A10 Écusson de parachutiste.

A11 Écusson de combat de char d'assaut de Luftwaffe. Type de base établi en novembre 1944 manqua le petit cartouche au-dessus, illustré ici: ce montra le numéro de combats—25, 50 et 75.

A12 Brassard du régiment 'General Göring' porté de mars 1936. Troupes portèrent brassards avec lettres grises. Brassards de sous-officiers avec lettres grises et tuyautage, brassards d'officiers avec lettres argentées et tuyautage. Ce brassard fut encore un usage occasionel dans la guerre avancée.

A13 Brassard divisionnaire 'Hermann Göring' porté brièvement de mai 1942.

A14 Brassard divisionnaire 'Hermann Göring' lequel remplaça le modèle préalable après quelques mois. Troupes portèrent lettres grises claires, officiers lettres argentées et tuyautage argenté.

B Entretien d'officiers Panzer, L'Italie 1943

Estafette porte complet d'aviateur comme combinaison d'automobilisme; motocyclette BMW R75/A1 tient insignes du bataillon de reconnaissance sur garde-boue. À gauche du groupe est un Hauptmann mis en tenue de Panzer noire avec calot, brassard de dessin d'officier, insignes du col blancs et pattes d'épaules avec tuyautage rose. À côté de lui est un beau Leutnant portant en partie tenue de service de Luftwaffe bleue, en partie tenue de Panzer noire avec insignes du col noirs avec tuyautage blanc. Le troisième officier porte vêtements de camouflage du dessin de SS sur sa tenue de Panzer noire. Le quatrième, un Leutnant du bataillon d'artillerie automoteur porte une version spéciale Luftwaffe-bleue de tenue réglementaire de ce rameau et la casquette de 1943 avec tuyautage argenté. Prenez note d'insignes de 'crâne' epinglés directement au col. Le char d'assaut est le PzKpfw III avec marquages de Compagnie générale, 2ème Bataillon, Rgt. Panzer 'HG'.

C Pièce d'Artillerie Flak 88mm, L'Italie 1943

Dans la chaleur d'été les servants sont mis en partie en tenue des tropiques de distribution de Luftwaffe, en partie mis en vêtements de sport. L'officier porte le bonnet 'Meyer' et tenue des tropiques réglementaire avec le tuyautage rouge du régiment flak. Les insignes de la 2ème (grosse) Batterie sont peints sur l'affût. Les projectiles sont 'Sprengranate Patronen L/4.5'.

D Flak légère en action, L'Italie, 1943–44

À gauche est un autochenille SdKfz 10/4 montant un canon Flak 38 30mm; les servants portent vêtements de camouflage de dessin de SS sur tenues de service bleues de Luftwaffe. À droite est un autochenille SdKfz 251/7 aussi montant le Flak 38 avec servants mis en tenues de Panzer noires. Les insignes sur le véhicule identifient 10ème Batterie Flak (légère).

E Personnel divisionaire 'en sortie', L'Italie, 1944–45

Trois soldats s'amusent avec un jeu de 'skat' dans un café-restaurant italien. Gauche, un Unteroffizier mis en la Fliegerbluse beaucoup portée, son tuyautage blanc identifiant une unité de Grenadiers. En avant de janvier 1944 les insignes du col blancs furent remplacés des insignes des ailes de métal epinglés directement au col et le galon argenté de sous-officiers fut remplacé de galon gris. Milieu, un Unterfeldwebel mis en tenue de 'promenade' se composante de tunique de service de Luftwaffe avec quatre poches, casquette et pantalon. La Waffenfarbe jaune et l'écusson sur bras identifient une fraction à transmissions. Droite, un Gefreiter mis en tenue des tropiques. Son brassard de premier dessin et son écusson de parachutiste l'identifie comme un des Fallschirmjäger mis à la poste de la division tout au début de la carrière de la division.